My Untold Story

Felicia Newkirk

Copyright © 2023 by Seazons Collections Publishing House.

Copyright © 2023 by Scirocca Publication.

Copyright © 2023 by Felicia Newkirk

All rights reserved. No part of this book may be reproduced or used in any manner without written permission of the copyright owner.

"Breaking Chains, Embracing Me: My Journey to Freedom at 43."

Table of Contents

Chapter 1: Day One — 1

Chapter 2: First Love — 7

Chapter 3: Mommy First — 15

Chapter 4: Damn! I'm Grown — 18

Chapter 5: God Help Me — 21

Chapter 6: The Flaw to The Flawless — 28

Chapter 7: Change — 35

Chapter 8: My Husband in Disguise — 40

Chapter 9: Just Me — 44

Chapter 10: Chapter 43 — 47

Chapter 1

Day One

"I'm sorry Mrs. Newkirk, but one of you aren't going to make it! This is a high risk pregnancy! We are taking a chance!" Those were the words that left the doctor's mouth. But God saw otherwise. On November 30th, 1980 a beautiful, healthy baby girl was born. That's right! Me! Juanita and Jerry Newkirk welcomed little old me into this world. Not only did I live, but so did my strong mother. From the moment my parents laid eyes on me, they knew it was something special about me.

Growing up as far back as I can remember, I had a two parent childhood. Even though it seemed like they hated each other guts, they took care of their kids. My parents used to play spades every weekend. I use to love when the weekend came. That meant we're eating pizza or fried fish on Friday and Saturdays nights. My mom used to love to cook when company would come over. She loved feeding people. She would even give you the groceries out of our freezer if you didn't have any food at your house. My mom was a big giver. A woman with a big heart, I must admit. She believed that's how she got her blessings. But my dad hated it.

Moving forward…I remember when I was in the fifth grade. I think that's when my life changed. The school had a talent show that my parents allowed me to participate in. That's when I discovered I couldn't dance. Then there was my first fight; which was with a boy. But not any boy, "the boy" of the class. I was sitting in my desk, minding my own business trying to look cute. You know, the typical girl thing to do. Then all of a sudden, other kids were thumping each other with pencils. So one of them thumped "the boy" and he thought it was me. He got up in my face yelling then he pushed me.

Why he wanted to do that? I think I turned into someone else. I began swinging like I was fighting for my life. I was picking things up throwing them at him; including the desk. Yes, the desk! The kids were in the background making their chanting noises. Some were boosting it up and others were laughing. The next thing I know, I was in the office and they were calling my mother. My mother was not the lady to call. She believed in a saying that goes, "Where you show out at, you gonna get it at."

I wish they would've called my dad. My mother is one you don't want to come out to the school. It didn't matter what it was. You were wrong because she had to get off her job to come to your school. However, I didn't get a whooping that day. I was surprised. I got punished. Thanks to my dad; I was his little angel. But I still couldn't believe I beat the little boy up. I'm talking not a scratch on me. Nonetheless, fifth grade was a year like no other for me. It was my first everything.

Then Christmas came around. I got my first pair of riding boots. I don't know if y'all remember those or not, but I do. The ones that come up to your knee. I remember it like it was yesterday. I was with my mother and my sister in the mall. We were shopping because Christmas was in two days. After going to a million different stores, we finally went inside the store that I knew those riding boots were in. I didn't want nothing for Christmas but those boots! We walked through the shoe aisle and we found my sister her size first. She tried them on, and they looked perfect. So, I'm thinking we're about to get my size next, but my mother proceeded to the cashier to checkout. I stopped her and told her that I wanted the boots too and that's all I wanted. But she still didn't get them. I remember crying so hard, that I couldn't breathe. I didn't understand why I couldn't get the boots and my sister got them. I couldn't and I can't even remember the reason why I couldn't get the boots. It just didn't make any sense to me.

So, we made it home and I'm still heartbroken that I didn't get the boots. When my dad came home, he asked what was wrong with me. I told him with tears running down my face and snot bubbles coming out of my nose, head hurting, and with a depressed spirit that Mom didn't buy me the riding boots that I wanted for Christmas and that's all that I wanted. He and my mother had an exchanged words. Moments later he came where I was.

"Come on!" He said.

We got in the car and we went to the mall. We walked in the store that the boots were in and he got them for me. I was the happiest kid in the world. It was the happiest day of my life, but also the worse because I went against my mother. From that day on, I knew the love my dad had for me was different from what my mother had for me. I didn't understand it, but I felt it deep down in my soul.

The next thing I knew, my mom and dad went from hating each other, to really hating each other. I remember all the fights they had. From staying with some of my mom's friends to staying in a boarding houses; where I thought for some reason the men there was going to rape or kill us in our sleep. It was scary. The next morning we was on the way to Cairo, Georgia. Which is where my mother's, mother lived. This was my mom's hometown. She was done with Atlanta and my daddy. My brother stayed in Atlanta with some of his close friends. Eventually, he got into some trouble and got arrested.

That stressed my mom out even more; on top of her leaving Atlanta. That took a lot from us. She made sure she took care of him even if we were lacking on the outside because she felt he needed her more on the inside. We really went through a lot with my mom being the only provider. We went from not missing nothing to missing all the holidays. No school clothes, no birthdays, no lights, no hairdo's, or no new shoes. In other words, we went from sugar to shit! But I can say, she kept our clothes that we did have, clean. She did not play that! She made sure they were clean. We never wore dirty clothes. That's when my sister and I learned to do our own hair; which was the fan ponytails. We both knew that mom was only doing the best that she could and she never gave up.

Chapter 2

First Love

So, here I am in Cairo, Georgia at my grandmother's house. I was afraid of my grandmother; she was so mean. But my grandfather was the sweetest man alive. We used to stay up late and shit just to sit to the table in the kitchen to wait on him to take a shower. Then he would drag his feet down the long hallway to the kitchen. He loved chocolate, vanilla and strawberry ice-cream and we did too. I think this was the way to say sweet dreams to the kids every night. That was the best part about living at my grandparents house. My grandfather didn't miss a night without eating ice-cream. Then we moved out...

My Untold Story

My mom got her own place. It was only my sister and I. So, we shared a room. I didn't mind because I was scared to sleep alone anyway. There were nights that I knew my mom was still dealing with the fact that she left my dad because she started drinking very heavy. I am talking about drinking like I never saw it before and some would say, like a fish. My sister and I were really good girls, so we didn't stress her out. We avoided adding more stress on her. When the holidays and birthdays came around, they started passing us by, like it was just another day. That's when I realized that our lives went from sugar to shit. It was a major change! The sad part about it was, we couldn't do anything about it. We were just young kids. I missed my dad so much. But I love my mom no matter what.

Now time has passed and I am in the eighth grade and my sister is at the high school; she's in the 10th. I used to get out of school about twenty minutes before her. My school was walking distance from home. My sister used to have to ride the bus. After school, I would go to the bus stop and wait on her to get off of the bus before I go home so we could walk together.

On this particular day, my eyes landed on someone. I think the sun was shining in his direction. My eyes landed on him when he got off the bus laughing with a beautiful smile and big lips. His forehead was shining off the sun. Last, but not least, he had broad shoulders and strong arms like I've never seen them before. I was melting. Then he walked past me. I think I stopped breathing because he spoke. Next thing I remember is my sister pushing me. "Come on girl. What are you doing?" She asked.

My mouth wouldn't move. I couldn't explain the experience I've just had. I was in a daze for a second. "Felicia!" She called out. Then boom, I snapped out of my trance.

"Who is that?" I asked her.

"Girl, nobody!" She said dryly.

"He's so cute. Can you please introduce me to him." I begged.

"No! That boy too old for you." She said. But I

wasn't hearing that. I couldn't stop thinking about him. He was so fine. He had really blown my mind. I didn't care what my sister said, I was going to make it my business to find out just who he was.

A few months past and guess what? We started talking as friends. We didn't ask each other if we wanted to be together, it just happened. Over the summer he started coming to the house. He met my mom and he started chilling with me everyday. Then it came to the point where he wanted more from me. I felt as if, if I didn't give him what he wanted, I was going to loose him. So, I put my big girl panties on and lost my virginity. I couldn't believe it. It wasn't all bad like my friends used to say. But after that, it was nonstop. Every chance we got, we were like rabbits.

Then one day, I started feeling sick and noticed a lump in my belly that wasn't moving. It was a few month since I had seen a cycle and I didn't even notice it. I started wearing a big jacket to cover up my stomach because it was growing bigger and bigger by the day. Folks at the school started asking me if I was pregnant.

"Girl you look pregnant." Someone said.

"I'm not." I said punching my stomach in hopes of proving a point. But that didn't stop my stomach from growing bigger and bigger.

As the months past, I'm seven months pregnant without knowledge of knowing I were. Everyone was still telling me I was pregnant and of course, I'm still in denial. "You need to go to the doctor just to see!" Someone mentioned.

I was to afraid. What if I were? What would happen? So many thoughts went through my mind. I am young. I can't be pregnant! I blocked that thought completely out of my mind. It wasn't possible. Well at least, that's what I thought or wanted to believe.

Then one day my sister was with her boyfriend and told my mom that she was pregnant. My mom was so mad but not like I thought she would be. So, I knew it was time for me to come clean.

"Ma, I have something to tell you." I said.

"What is it?" She asked.

"I'm pregnant too." I admitted. She blew the roof off the place! But I was too far along and it was nothing that we could do.

After I had my baby, I moved out into an apartment with my child's father. We were doing good. I thought I was in heaven. I was going to school, working and being a mother. I was playing my full role. I was cooking and cleaning for the man I loved so much; and don't forget we on each other like white on rice. It was good for a while, then he started hanging out late not returning my 911 pages. We didn't really have phones. It was pagers and the house phone.

One night we were home and he had a few friends over. I was in the room and I fell asleep. Not long after I dosed off, some kind of way I woke up. I didn't feel him in the bed and I didn't hear him talking in the living room. I got up and looked out the front door. No one was there. I went to the kitchen and the door was cracked open. I heard moaning from a female's voice. I grabbed a knife out of my dish rack and quietly walked towards the door. What I saw, made me lose it. I dropped the knife and started throwing hands on him and the girl that he was on my back porch having sex with. She jumped off of the porch, which was twelve feet high. She was running for her life. I ran to the front door to see which way she had went. I did not see her anywhere. I ran back in the house to deal with his ass.

"Baby, I'm sorry! I'm sorry! I'm so, so sorry!" He pleaded.

"Why in the hell you was on my back porch with another girl? Why! Why would you do this to me!" I yelled.

"Baby, I don't know why I did it. I can't even tell you." He said.

"Oh you don't know why! Ok! Stay right there!" I began throwing everything I could get my hands on at him; including these hands.

The pain I was feeling, I couldn't explain. I couldn't come back from that. I stayed there about a week and I got my baby and we went back to my mother's house. That was the end of that. I knew I didn't deserve it. I was only seventeen years old. I was trying to live with him, thinking it was going to work. But love didn't live here anymore.

Chapter 3

Mommy First

Now I am back at my mother's house. My mom had a two bedroom trailer. So, me, my sister and our babies shared a room. My mom gave us the master bedroom. It was a lot of room in there for a queen size and a twin size bed. I had the twin size. I really slept in the queen because I always had my sister's baby with me also. It was me, my little girl and my niece. Keep in mind, I'm only seventeen years old. And you won't believe it, but I'm four months pregnant with my second child from my first love.

So, one day I got a call that my dad was in town and he was coming by. I was always excited to see him because we would laugh and talk about everything. I was waiting on him to pull up. I was on the porch. We sat out there for about two hours talking about life. "Live your life baby girl." He said. He didn't know I was really trying, but I was running into stones along the way.

Now the summer is here and I have had my baby. I'm ready to go back to school and finish these last two years. I made arrangements to drop the kids off with their father while I go to school and pick them back up after school. Their father was no longer in school, so I thought that would be a great way for me to just go and finish my last two years.

As the weeks go by, everything going great. Then I started to have to find a babysitter in the mornings to drop the kids off before I can go to school. Some of his family was trying to help watch them when I couldn't find him in the morning. But all I needed was a babysitter from eight to three, Monday through Friday so that I could go to school and finish. I started missing days when I couldn't find him. One day I pulled up to drop them off and it was weird. I walked in and I was given instructions as I was sitting my kids down on the chair. In the house, there was a high sofa that sits up off the floor. I was able to see what was under it. And someway, I looked down and seen a plate with white stuff on it. I wasn't dumb to the streets. I knew exactly what it was. I grab my kids and I looked at him. "Never mind. I will keep them. I don't want them in this mess that you got going on!"

"Man I'm not keeping them no more!" He yelled.

"That's fine with me!" I assured him.

I went home and cried my eyes out. All I wanted was to finish school and that was the day I had to quit. My mom worked so she wasn't able to sit home and keep my children plus pay her bills. My sister had a babysitter for her kids. So that left me at home. I was seventeen years old with two kids and a drop-out. But, I had to be a mommy first.

Chapter 4

Damn! I'm Grown

I'm eighteen years old now and you can't tell me nothing. I'm working at Taco Bell. My sister is helping me by watching the kids. We stay together now and she work overnights. So when I am not working, I have the kids. Now my sister gets closer with her baby daddy and he moves in. So, you know what that leaves me? Back with my mom or find us somewhere to go. I really didn't want to be a burden on anyone. I was with my mother some nights and I also had a close friend that had her on, so I stayed there some nights. At this point, I was applying for an apartment. It was months before it came along. But I was grateful, so I moved in. For the first time,

I felt complete.

I wasn't used to being alone. So, all of my friends used to come hang out at my spot because everyone my age still was staying with their mother or parents. My house was the getaway. Over time, I learned how to survive. The streets taught me that it's no love out here in these streets. I was finding myself doing whatever I had to do to make sure my kids and I had the things we needed. My mother couldn't help me. My sister was living her life. My baby daddy didn't give a fuck in the world. But here I am at nineteen years old now with two kids and one on the way. Yep I let him hit it one more time.

But anyways, time goes by and it's now my daughters birthday. I cooked hotdogs, fries and we had a cake. The day went good. During this time, my sister and her kids were staying with me. The kids was in one room playing and I was in the living room laying down. Out of nowhere, I hear the children yelling, screaming, and crying to the top of their lungs. I jumped up and opened the door. It was a fire in the room. I grabbed all of the keys out of the room. We rushed outside on the sidewalk and called the police and fire department. They came and put out the fire. The kids had got a hold of the cake lighter. The one with a push of a button that lights. But just like that, I didn't have a place to stay. After that, it was one thing after another. There was plenty of nights I didn't remember nights. I sold drugs to the hood and sold pussy to the dope boys. I had to do what ever I had to do to make sure my kids didn't have to let holidays and birthdays pass them by. So when I say by any means, I meant by any means. I stayed with friends, family, my mother and at rooms; just where ever I could. Until one day, I saw a house that was just right for me and my kids. I did what I had to do to come up with the money. The next thing you know, I was moving in. I had a friend at the time. He was younger than me, but he was in love with me. When he saw me moving in the house, he was excited. He was getting comfortable but I told him no one is staying at my house if you not paying bills. From that day on, I never paid a bill. He stepped in and took that weight off of me.

Chapter 5

God Help Me

Well, I have been going through a lot and also praying a lot. I'm twenty one years old and I have three kids. I'm just trying to find a way. I was with a friend and her friend had a friend that wanted to talk to me. So I said ok, but he wasn't my type. He was nice and he wasn't giving up. So we went on a double date. It was nice; I enjoyed it. We went back to my friends and chilled. After that, we talked every day. He did not miss a day without calling me. I started seeing him more often. At this point, we didn't say we were together. But we were surely working on it. During this time, I was staying with my friend. After two weeks there, I found a house that I loved. It was in a great area. I called the man who owned the house and asked him if I could see it. When I got there to look at the house, it was everything I needed. The owner assured me, it was all mine if I wanted it. I gave him the money for the house.

Next, I just had to get my lights on. I didn't have it and I asked everyone I knew to see if I can get the money up fast as I could. Once again, I found myself having to do whatever it took to get this money so me and my kids can have somewhere to stay. I made a phone call later that day. I met up with him. And I did what I had to do to get the money. The next day I was moving in. My friend at the time was excited for me. He came over to see the place. I was back in my own space and I enjoyed it very much. I was doing hair and whatever else I needed to do to make sure my daughters was straight. But with this friend had turned into my man, my man, my man. He was right there with me and made sure I didn't have to worry about nobody else or things my daughters needed. He was the best man I have ever had. God sent me exactly what I wanted and needed in my life. We were together for twelve years and this man never changed on me. He was always giving me what I needed. He didn't have any kids of his own, but he raised my girls like they were his very own. When I say myself, and my daughters didn't want for anything, that's just what I meant. I made sure that he didn't want for anything either. It even came to the point where I didn't even need child support from their father. Even though he wasn't paying it. Christopher told me to leave him alone, he's here now! I didn't need him. And that's what I did. I thought that was the realist thing I had ever heard. He stood on his word and still does.

Overtime, we was the city Bonnie and Clyde. It was me and Christopher together no matter what. We did everything together and he always loved to make sure we had the kids. We never had to get a babysitter because he wanted everyone to see that he had a family. They loved him. He was my best friend, my lover, my man, my everything. One thing I can say, we grew up together. We both were young, but had big dreams and did whatever it took to get it. Money was never a problem. We both were hustlers. Then somewhere down the line things got rocky! We were breaking up, dating other people and then we would get back together. It was crazy love. But this one particular time, this girl stated she was pregnant from him. I lost my mind. We didn't have kids and someone is saying that she will be having his baby. I could not take that at all. I was thinking things were going to change the way he was with me and my daughters. I told him I don't want you to go through that. So just go be with your baby mama. He didn't want to, but I seen his face that he was happy about someone being pregnant from him.

A month passed and I heard she lost the baby. I can't say I didn't feel a sense of relief. He was calling and begging to come back home. Yes, I let him come. But from that point on, he wasn't the same. We were fussing more than ever. He would leave and go hang out with some of his friends a lot. One night I got a call that he was in trouble and going to jail. I couldn't believe it. Then they gave him two years once he went to court. The two years didn't seem that long, but it was the longest ever. We wasn't together when he went in, but I stood by him the whole time he was in there. I took care of him. He didn't need nothing from no one else. I made sure his books were straight and I never missed a visit. I visit him every two weeks and I even remember the holidays. The faculty staff let us bring real food to the inmates. We ate good. I made him feel like he was a King. I made him everything he wanted. I took this time to show him how much I appreciated him for coming into my life and being the man that he was for me and my kids. So when it came to the day he got released, I told him that he don't owe me anything. I took care of him because of what he did for me. Not for him to think that he is obligated or owe me anything. But he said, "OK but I want to be with you."

So we gave it another try. During this time I had moved to a new city; Tallahassee Florida. I was getting on my feet. I brought him home with me to a three bedroom plus three bath townhome. He was there for about six months. He didn't like it and we started arguing. Things didn't go well. I told him I don't want him to feel pressured to stay. One day, we got into an argument and I told him to call him a ride to go back to Georgia. He thought it was going to be a little disagreement, but I knew this was the end. I wasn't in love with him anymore. And during the time he was away, I had time to think to myself. My kids were getting older. He wanted kids of his own but I knew I didn't want anymore. I felt that I was being selfish. So I knew I had to let him go so he could build his own family with someone else in order for him to be happy in life. This was one of the hardest things I had to ever do in my life. It hurt me to my core, but I knew I was doing the right thing.

Now a year and a half has passed. He's with some new girl and she is pregnant. I was so happy for him even though we were no longer together. I was so happy for him. Then two years later, he got another baby. I stayed in touch with him after the break up. When I talked to him, I used to always tell him that if his kids need anything and I mean anything, I got them. I even tried to meet his baby mothers, but they wasn't having it. They wasn't mature enough yet for that. So, I just let him know all the time that I got him if he ever needs me. And still to this day, he is in love with me and ready to rekindle our relationship.

Chapter 6

The Flaw to The Flawless

Well here I am living in Florida with my three daughters. I am new to the city, so I want to see everything. I was hanging out almost every day because there was always something to do. So one night me and my sister went out to the club, to meet a friend of hers. The place was packed when we got there. We was drinking and dancing all night. I was headed to the bar and this guy asked if I drink Vodka. I said, "Yes I do."

"You can have some of mine if you want." He had a whole bottle of Ciroc. He had just bought it, so I said sure.

"Does your sister want a cup also?" He asked.

"Yes." My sister said. So I poured us a cup. We introduced ourselves to each other. We were chilling and dancing for the rest of the night. The guys watched us the rest of the night. The one name Thomas was looking at me with a glare in his eyes.

Now the club is over. Thomas asked if he could get my number. I said yes because he had been so kind and he didn't bother me the rest of the night about that drink. He called me the same night. We talked until I got home then I said goodnight. The next day, I had to work and I talk to him before work. I told him I get off at 8p.m. so I will talk to him then. I got off at 8:01 p.m. and my phone rings. It was him. He asked to take me out to a spot to watch the basketball game. I said sure. I went home, got dressed and met him at the spot. It was thick in there. We had some drinks and food as we talked. I learned about basketball, of course. From that day on, I saw him every day.

He took me to go meet his mother. I was shocked because I only knew him for about a week. He took me out to a lot of places. Thomas even started going to his hometown which was forty-five minutes away. He didn't care what we were doing, as long as I was with him. Time passed and he started staying the night at my house but he wouldn't touch me. So I was wondering what was going on with him. One night I did the butt push move on him until he had to grab this ass. It went down from there. He moved in and we were together for the next four years. Then come to find out the car he was driving was his BabyMomma's which he lied and said it was his little sister. He gave the car back and we kept on dating. At one point, I had moved to his hometown with him. I was there so much. We had a lot of good times together. Until this day, I think I was his trophy girl. He use to love showing me off to his friends. Hell to anyone. I was fine, fine. We were together so much until he literally was my everything. We used to laugh, fuss, fight and fuck. He started getting plenty of money. Now here comes the hoes. That's what money and a bad bitch will get you. Then we broke up because he started back dealing with his baby mother. Which I thought he was out of town working for four years. How dumb! But he had to deal with her in order to see his child. We all know how that go. Then there was other women in his hometown that wanted him back that he used to deal with in his past. So I let him go on about his business.

After a year we started back being friends. I think I only slept with him two or three times after we wasn't together. We talked all day, every day on the phone for hours. He used to buy me lunch and sometimes I used to buy him lunch. He was really my best friend. I've talk to him about a lot of things; even my relationship that I currently had after him. I trusted him with my life that's how close I thought we were. I remember he got in an accident and his sister called me to tell me. I was at work and when I say I dropped everything to get to the hospital to see him. Then when I realize that he was ok and he had to go in surgery that it would be a while before I see him, that's when I thought to myself…..why am I here? This is not my man. I knew then that I loved this man.

I got into another relationship and all, but we

still remained friends. So when my relationship was over, I turned more to him, which was the closest person to me at this time. We hung out a lot, but we wasn't sleeping around. So one day he said, "I want to take you to Cali."

"Really?" I was so excited but I really didn't think we were going so I brushed it off. But we did a road trip and it was beautiful to see all the mountains, snow and different animals. The ride was awesome. California was like a movie. He took me everywhere there. I took pictures on every corner. It was a beautiful place and I couldn't believe I was there. I did all the eating and shopping a girl could do. I got high and I don't smoke or do any drugs at all. So you know I was high for days. I really enjoyed myself. I didn't want to leave. Then a few months passed, we went to Cali again. But this time, it was different. His homeboy was with us. It was weird but I went with it anyway becauseI was with Thomas so I felt ok. We were on the way back, I was driving and all of a sudden I was feeling sleepy. We switch seats. I was in the back laying down and could not keep my eyes open. After a few moments,

I'm being awaken by Thomas. He says he was being pulled over. I sat up and looked around as I wipe my eyes. Then over comes the officer to the car. The officer asked for the driver which was Thomas friend for his license and registration. Then he told the driver to get out for a minute. Then the officer came back to the driver side and asked the passenger which was, Thomas and myself in the backseat could he search the car. We both said no. Then the officer told us to get out of the car. So now we standing on the side of the road in handcuffs. They got the dogs out and started searching the vehicle. They picked up my purse, which had my handgun in it. He asked who it belongs to, I said me Sir and I'm license it to carry it. He put it to the side. Then he pops the trunk and opened up bags. He started pulling out stuff.

"Who this belong to?" He asked

Thomas said what belonged to him. Thomas also told the officer to let me go. I had nothing to do with what was going on. The officer pulled out more stuff and ask who it belong to. No one said anything. I looked at Thomas friend, he looked down at the ground. I knew then shit had just got real. He stood there and did not say a word. The officer at that time put me in the patrol car and took all of us to jail. So now I'm pissed and ready to get my phone call. I have seen shit like this on a movie before but I never been in trouble before. I do think he was supposed to say something. So now I'm in this little country town with no Black people. I'm about to freak out because this man looked at the ground. I get on the phone with my daughter and she states that a friend had told her that Thomas friend told someone back home that if things didn't go right, he was putting everything on me. I went off in the jail and told him that's bullshit and he has to do the right thing.

Now I am back-and-forth to Texas for court for two years. I went my whole life doing good and surrounded myself with genuine people. I wait until I get forty years old to hang with the wrong flaw ass crowd. I'm too old for this bullshit! Those were my thoughts to myself.

Chapter 7

Change

This was a big change for me as well as my kids. I moved to Florida to get a new start and took a fresh breath of air. It was different. It was just me and my daughters. I didn't have a man but I can say I picked a great spot. Everyone was so nice and the neighbors communicated with each other. The day we moved, the neighbors were having a block party for all the people in the neighborhood. They even helped me move in. I didn't have to unload the truck at all. They took all the heavy stuff in the house for me. I was thankful because I was so tired already from making two trips. Then instead of unpacking, we took a bath and were outside so we could meet

My Untold Story

and mingle with the new neighbors. It was nice. From that day on, I've been cool with everyone from the hood. I was already working, so that was a great thing. But it was way more expensive than it was in Georgia. But I seem to manage with God on my side. I was struggling for a few months, then I got the hang of everything. It was flowing from there. Being new in town and people not knowing my face, they didn't want to tell you nothing. You had to find out on your own. So I started hanging out so I could get to know people. I met a lot of good people also. But you know there's always a snake in the grass when you're dealing with females. So myself and Shay were getting close. I was at her house all the time for her functions and parties. I introduced her to the guy I was talking to. She didn't like him for me. Of course I was too good for him she said. Then I had a friend that I introduced her too and she called him my other dude name. I knew then what kind of shit that was. But luckily, I had told him about my other dude anyway.

Then I was friends with this other guy and I asked him did he know her. He said, "Yes, I tried to talk to her but it didn't go nowhere."

I asked her about the dude and she snapped. "He ain't no good, girl. He's a liar! Girl, you don't need to talk to him!"

But she didn't say it went nowhere. So I continued to talk to him because I wanted to get to know people for myself. One day, I get a call from him. I missed it of course. I was busy but then she called me, so I answered it. "Girl I told you he wasn't no good. He tried me last night. I told him I love you and I won't do nothing like that to you. I told him he was a dirty motherfucker for trying me and he knows I be with you!" She said.

"Oh wow! But ok, that's what's up. I will call you back a little later because I'm still busy." I said.

I called him to see what he had to say. He asked me did I talk to her? I said yes and I told him what she said. Then he said, "She is mad because I won't give her money and the day you asked her about me, she got in my inbox and started texting me, asking me for money in messenger. Yes, I did give her money twice. I bet she didn't tell you. She showed me her coochie piercing."

"No, she didn't tell me that. But whatever y'all got going on, y'all can have it. Leave me out of it!"

I stop talking to both of them but when I see them, I do speak; but that's all. I started hanging out alone or with my grown daughters and their husbands. I don't have time for the new friend thing. I was going great. I had no problems in life right now.

One night, I was in one of the bars I hung at. It was thick that night. I was looking like a million dollars. I am the type person that always stand out in the crowd. I was walking into the bar with my little sister and we sat down. Then I seen the guy I have been watching for a while, but never got a chance to introduce myself. I told my sister that I was going to walk over there and be noticed by him. So I did. I brushed up against him and said excuse me. He was talking to the waiter. We were standing really close, so he was looking in my face. But before I could speak, my sister was over there.

"Hey! What's your name and are you here

alone?"

"Yes!" He answered.

"Well this is my sister and I think y'all should meet each other." She was very direct.

I was so shame but we've been good friends ever since then. But this particular night, Shay was there and she saw us talking. She threw salt on my name. But at this point, I definitely didn't go by what she said. I hit him up the next day. He told me what she said. I couldn't believe it. I told him what she said about him. We still began our friendship and we were good friends. I was used to haters but not snakes right up under my nose. So that was the end of speaking to her. Goodbye, Shay!

Chapter 8

My Husband in Disguise

Well, well, well! Where do I begin with this one? I met him on social media. We were chatting for a minute and then we finally got a chance to meet up with each other. When I first laid eyes on him, I was in disbelief. This man was tall, dark, handsome, with a pretty smile, fine as hell, and a beard. And to top it all off, it's red head. I knew that God had answered my prayers. He didn't have much, but I didn't mind it. I helped him do things he needed to better himself. He opened my mind up to the business world. And I haven't turned back since. He had a little girl about seven years old at that time and she was so beautiful just like him. We started seeing each other every day until we was in a relationship. He was always saying he wasn't ready for a relationship but one day he started, calling me his lady. So, I didn't mind that at all. Then I met his family and he met mine. We were raised differently, but I didn't think nothing of that either. I have always said everybody go through things in life. That's why it's called life. Now he has a good job and we staying together and taking trips. Life was great. Our sex life was the bomb. He took the time to know my whole body. I have never been in love like this before and he showed me that he loved me because he was doing things for me that he said he has never done before for a woman. We were so in love. Now I was waiting on him to ask me to marry him. I started asking questions and he started pulling away. Everyone use to ask us are we getting married and I would be saying I hope so because I'm ready, I'm waiting on him.

But as time went by, things started changing. I started catching him in lies. He had cheated on me several times, and I forgave him because he said he loves me. I started praying for God to reveal to me if he was for me. Was he really my husband or just not for me? I started talking to his brother wife at the time. Him and her was going through things. Then one day we was talking and she was telling me a story about her and my mother-in-law at the time. She was naming everyone that was there and she said Map Wife. I said, "What did you say? Who wife?"

So she repeated it and my heart was broken into pieces at this time. I couldn't believe she just said Map wife. He never told me he was married. This was a dealbreaker for me. I told him I don't talk to married men because I feel some type of way about that. As I waited until he got home from work, I was in disbelief. We showered and sat on the bed. I asked him about marrying me he said yes, he do want to marry me. So I asked him about the wife and he got so mad about me knowing. He left the house and did not come back all night. I was like, wait a minute it's not that serious for you to stay out all night. Then he started arguments just to stay out all night. I found out he was out there doing drugs and having sex for money. I was disgusted at this point, but was still trying to act like he love me. I tried to get him some help but he didn't want it. We were arguing everyday.

One night, we get into it and he swung at me. Me and my daughter was there at the time and I had to fight him. Her friend called the police. He got his daughter and left the house. But he had took my gun with him. With him being in trouble before, he was not supposed to have it. It was a big mess, but I got my gun back. He went to jail and I was free from this person I thought I could spend the rest of my life with. My God said different. I was happy when he moved him out of my life because he didn't mean me no good.

Chapter 9

Just Me

Well, here I am at the age of forty-two. I feel like I'm at my prime. I am more on the business side of my life. It seems like I'm just now figuring things out. I am single because I'm waiting on my husband to find me this time. God send me my Boaz. Yes, it gets lonely, but this time being alone has giving me time to work on me. I'm eating better. Trying to put exercise in my daily routine. I have a clear mind on everything in life right now. I now have three businesses. I enjoy all of them. I am stress-free and I must say, I know what peace is now. And I don't want anyone to disturb it. I want to keep this feeling for the rest of my life; rather I'm with someone or not. I have locked my hair up. I love it. I think that was one of the best moves I have ever done also. Is now been four years. It'll be five by the time I finish this book. I love them and everyone else always complements my hair. To be honest, I really didn't think I would make it this far on my lock journey but I can say, my life started to change as my hair grew. I found myself more into me. I have no tolerance for bullshit. I am a true Sagittarius and I'll speak my mind. A lot of people can't deal or handle the truth, so they get mad at me. Even my own kids because they are grown now and I don't sugarcoat anything with them. I have three daughters that are grown, 28, 26 and 24.

One thing I can say, you will be surprised how your children really feel about you if they ever get a chance to tell you. You go along in life, not knowing the little things or simple things you have said or done has hurt someone deeply. But in reality, all you can do is apologize and keep moving forward. I have found myself doing just that. I apologize and move forward and that's all I can do. I can't turn back the hands of time and change anything. At the end of the day, I was a child, having children with no guidance. So yes, I was not perfect but I can say they had a great childhood. I did the best I could and I am patting myself on the back that I did it. So after giving them my life, I don't think I owe them anything else. I love them; don't get me wrong. But I'm not living in the past anymore. I'm focusing on my future. I'm sorry, but I am not sorry for my past. I really have no regrets. But I will say our relationship is a little different, because really we all grew up together. Sometimes I think they think we all are the same age, but in reality, I am the mother. So respect must be given. I don't think any mother should take disrespect from a child. You gave birth to them, but no one said you are perfect. But just like my mom always told me, "You will see what I'm talking about when you have kids."

Now two of them have kids and one doesn't. But they are in for the ride. With that all being said, I know I can never change the past, but I will always live for the future.

Chapter 10

Chapter 43

---◆---

It's a few months before my 43rd birthday. Well I must say, it has really been a journey and I'm talking about all forty-two years. I usually do something big for my birthday but this year, I want to take time out to reflect on me. From day one when I was born, the doctor said I wasn't going to make it. But I showed them! When God is on your side, anything is possible. From this little girl that grew up with her mother, not caring for her as much as the other children. From being a teenage mother at the age of fifteen, even having to be a mommy first, choosing the kids over myself, the long nights that I had to endure with different men

My Untold Story

for money. Even the times I was even taken for granted and the days I had to figure out no one wanted their child to be around me because I had children as a child. Don't forget the single mother stage because their father didn't want anything to do with them. To the fact my mother wasn't able to take care of me and my kids. I put him on child support and he stated, he would go to prison before he does for my kids. That day, he marked his own life. Even the days I had to cry and beg for diapers and milk. I even had to go to strangers. Even the time I had a friend that used me to only benefit for herself out of it; that's from a so-called friend. The days I wanted to just break down and cry because no one cared for me. The times I had to take kids to work with me just to work. The days I had to make things happen because no one else did. The times I had to trick with a man just to get school clothes for my kids. The days I sold illegal products. To the days I have done illegal things to pay bills.

All the days I reset my life for them, but when I say, God gets all the glory for bringing me through it. All the horrible relationships, especially the one

I was facing charges with at the age of forty. Bu God gets all the glory for bringing me through and keeping my mind for the days of court I had to attend and traveling back-and-forth to court in Texas. From the moments when I wasn't even there in court and my name being mentioned and the prosecutor say don't mention her name no more.

Thank you for being a shield for me God. I thank you and you get all the glory. I walked away with a misdemeanor when I was facing felony charges. Even the two years, where I almost turned into an alcoholic fighting the thoughts in my mind.Lord, I thank you for all the courage. After all of that, I remained humble and full of faith. I thank God whom has always been ahead of my life. I thank him for all he has done, doing and is going to do in my life. I must say, this old life of mine has really made me the woman I am today. Which is a beautiful, ambitious, passionate, loving, caring, curvy, fine as wine, natural, happy, living, resilient, elegant, phenomenal, feminine, charming, visionary and funny me. If you get nothing else out of my book, please know that there is nothing God can't pull you thru.

Well, that's my story the end

As of November 30, 2023 I am 43 and free....

Made in the USA
Columbia, SC
09 October 2024